OXYGEN

Parables of the Pandemic

RIVER PAW PRESS

Oxygen: Parables of the Pandemic
Copyright © River Paw Press

First Edition: 2022

ISBN: 978-1-7366871-1-6

Concept, Anthology Selection and the Editor's Note
Copyright © Kalpana Singh-Chitnis, 2022

Individual Poems and Translations
Copyrights © Individual Poets and Translators

Layout, Book Cover © Silent River
Cover Photo: © Sirawich Rungsimanop (Public Domain)
Copy Editing: Kalpna Singh-Chitnis and Nirvan Chitnis

River Paw Press

USA

www.riverpawpress.com

OXYGEN

Parables of the Pandemic

Edited by

Kalpna Singh-Chitnis

River Paw Press

Acknowledgment

We want to thank all contributing poets and translators of
Oxygen:Parables of the Pandemic for their profound work and
Sirawich Rungsimanop for his outstanding photograph, which graces the cover
of this anthology. I also want to thank our managing editor Nirvan Chitnis
for his endless hours of work in putting this book together for us.

A very special thanks to Jack Foley, William O'Daly, Phyllis Becker,
Lois P. Jones, Susan Rogers, Mani Suri, Amata Natasha Goldie,
Megha Sood, Ruth Furtado, Stephenie Masek, Carol Ducey, Anil Chitnis,
Shashwat Chitnis, Vishwa Chitnis, and Nirvan Chitnis for their support
to our "Oxygen" project at River Paw Press through which we raised
substantial funds in 2021 for "GiveIndia" and "Project Hope"
non-profits, fighting COVID-19 in India.

For

My Mother

Prem Lata Singh

and

All the Victims and Survivors of the Coronavirus Pandemic

CONTENTS

Editor's Note

As I write this note for *Oxygen: Parables of the Pandemic,* the virus celebrates the newest addition to its family— Deltacron. According to the astrologers of medical science, the love child of Delta and Omicron is supposed to be the noblest among all known members of the COVID-19 family. What this phenomenon tells us is apparent. The virus is not going anywhere. It will stay with us, and we must learn to live with it.

We owe enormous gratitude to the scientists around the world for finding the vaccines that have saved millions of lives. We also owe the leaders who have understood the need to rise above political rivalries, selfish instincts and the boundaries of nations to come together to find solutions for diseases, hunger, and war, for the sake of humanity.

However, many world leaders do not seem committed enough to healing the planet. The pandemic was not enough for them to destroy the world, so the invasions of smaller countries must continue, and they must profit from the misery of humankind. The sunflower fields are charred, Ukraine is bleeding before our eyes, and we have allowed this to happen without guilt. It is heartbreaking and numbing.

Coronavirus outbreak shook the world to its core, and we helplessly watched our friends, family, and loved ones leave a little too soon, and the world economy destroyed, forcing millions into poverty and homelessness. It has been over two years since the virus was detected, but the hospitals are still admitting COVID19 patients worldwide, and people are dying of the virus and several health issues caused by it.

At the same time, we must not forget the courage and dedication of our doctors, nurses, and essential workers who have saved countless lives by risking their own since the pandemic struck. The generosity of the world community to help people in need of food, medicine, vaccines, and much more has shown the best of humanity.

It is only relevant to mention that I had booked my travel for Vietnam, Thailand, and South Korea in 2020, without knowing that an unprecedented event would soon change everything for the whole world in the most harrowing way. I was supposed to be in Hanoi, Hue, and at Plum Village in Thailand, with a group of Buddhist practitioners on a retreat and possibly meeting Zen master Thich Nhat Hanh. I was supposed to moderate a panel of writers at 2020 AWP in San Antonio before traveling abroad, but the pandemic dismantled every plan I had made.

The way the world events were unfolding, gripping lives with severity after the outbreak of the Coronavirus—literature, art, and meditation were the only things to anchor me safe on an isolated island of uncertainty, preventing me from drowning in despair. The most painful things were being separated from my children, not seeing my ailing mother in India in her final days, and attending her funeral, followed by emotional and financial setbacks. But I was not ready to give in to despair and turned my confinement at home into a retreat. I began to meditate on the impermanence of life more fervently than I ever did before. The result of this meditation brought me a sense of urgency and taught me to appreciate life more and more. I turned to nature and found extended joy in watching the sun, clouds, and rain. I delighted in speaking to birds and animals, feeding them, and caring for plants and trees. I cooked and ate the healthiest food, took Ayurvedic supplements, and continued with Yoga, which I have been practicing since childhood. I took upon things I always wanted to do but was not finding time for them.

The dreadful days of the pandemic renewed my commitments to life, and profoundly inspired my creativity, including conceptualizing a collection of poems on 'pandemics of the century' that later turned out to be "Oxygen: Parables of the Pandemic" focused on COVID-19 only. The concept of the anthology inspired the "Oxygen" project at River Paw Press, and I raised funds for "GiveIndia" and "Project Hope" to help COVID-19 victims in India. I also decided to turn some of my poems into films. My education in film directing at NYFA came into practice at a humbling time, and I selected a few verses from my poetry collection *Bare Soul* to translate them into moving images.

Little did I know, at that time, that I would survive the pandemic, and my poetry-film "River of Songs" and my poems would travel to the Moon in a time capsule, with NASA's missions in 2022 and 2023. Sometimes I'm fascinated by how the universe pours out its gifts to make up for our losses. The pandemic took many things away from us but also gave gifts in return. The gift of awareness of our wellbeing, the lesson to value life, and our relationship with our environment and the rest of the world.

Here I want to quote Vietnamese Zen master Thich Nhat Hanh, nominated for Nobel Peace Prize by Martin Luther King - *"The tears I shed yesterday have become rain."*

The works in this collection, like rain, water the seeds of our consciousness to break from the illusion of our separateness. In our fragile existence and sufferings, we are one and together. Together, we have created this anthology to dedicate our work to the world, so we can be aware of our neglect, celebrate the joy of our survival, and understand the importance of our mindful actions in saving our planet.

There is nothing profound in a calamity, but the lessons we derive from it and how we stand with courage and optimism in the face of adversities.

Kalpna Singh-Chitnis

Kalpna Singh-Chitnis

"I have no idea what's awaiting me, or what will happen when this all ends.

For the moment I know this: there are sick people and they need curing."

Albert Camus, *The Plague*

The Clock Strikes Quarantine,
and Life Learns a New Song

By Kelli Russell Agodon and Melissa Studdard

Which was really the song it knew all along
but forgot to sing as it stopped in awe to watch
the cars and jets whizzing past, the old song
of walks and telephone calls, a woman baking
bread with the window open, the empty calendar
song we now hum to, notes written to a friend,
I miss you. Life is no longer an orchestra's crescendo,
but softer, dolce, what we almost forgot existed,
the caesuras of us - we pause and with the silence
of highways, we finally hear the birds.

Sometimes Our Job is To Be Still

By Kelli Russell Agodon and Melissa Studdard

Between the birdsong and cloudsway, there's beauty.

Between a call from a friend and the hiss of the news,
how do we balance a life? An incomplete breakdown

at the dawn of a day, the rest meticulously to follow.

We're still climbing out of primordial soup with bodies
half human, half microbe. We're still trying to make sense

of stowaway DNA. Which means we cultivate compassion

from an heirloom starter. We examine our eyes and smiles
in mirrors: between microbiome and human, what peace?

Who nests in us? We are more like trees than we ever knew—

our job sometimes to be still, shelter in place, properly space
our rows—to love each other by bearing down, staying home.

We Lose Ourselves in Isolated Gardens, Find Each Other on Zoom

By Kelli Russell Agodon and Melissa Studdard

We play our violins for earthworms
and blue jays, scribble down the blue
jays' notes. When you Zoom me, I'll sing
the story I heard in the branches,
improvise the Stradivarius birds. They say
teenagers in isolation play ukulele until 1 a.m.
Sadness follows them like a moon
to their online prom. Outside,
nightbirds wear tuxedos until morning
when tassel-headed quail shuffle forward,
united, as if towards an invisible stage.

Forbidden Realm

By Dee Allen

Voluminous mountains
Dusted with snow,

Evergreens crowning hillsides, bristly branches maintain
Their colour in the time of cold & no growth,

Water projected upward in
Mad bursts as geysers

Or running downward over
Cliffs as perpetual falls,

Gorges and canyons, deep cracks
In the ground grown wider with age & erosion,

Freshwater lakes worth
Traveling on by boat, by paddle stroke or motor,

Sequoias in rows, gigantic, old-growth
Extra canopy for the tent-sleepers at the bases of trunks,

Families of different shades,
Different flora sprout in one area, forming a great garden

Are prohibited
To human entry.

Fear of some tiny
Debilitating germ

Has sealed off the miracles,
Half of nature from us.

The lush, pleasing half
We're allowed to see

On wall calendars
And subway billboards.

That fatal virus
Undermined our lives,

Forced us indoors to stay safe.
Government orders.

Front gates of a national
Park, padlocked and shut

Like an ancient belt for chastity,
Helping Mother Earth keep her purity.

And as she
Regenerates, we

Steal little moments masqued up,
Enjoying nature. One half

Navigated walking or riding a bike
With the scenery rolling past, whereas

The other half of nature
Is a realm forbidden

For us to cross
Except in our fondest dreams.

The Well of Grief

after David Whyte

By Lana Hechtman Ayers

The orange klezmer music of sun
nowhere to be seen,
today's atmospheric fog white as worry,
though somewhere else the hazel-colored wrens
sing on the still-green boughs
and in the distant bluest seas
great orcas sing songs of long generations,
but here in my county of dread
the refrigerated morgue truck pulls up
behind the hospital for the newly COVID dead
whose numbers exceed normal storage capacity.

Red-as gore-illuminated sirens
are the sorrow songs
of this too-long pandemic.

Summer nearly gone,
the elation of blooms has faded
to solemn hymns,
broken only by thunderous cracks of rifle strikes
from the forest at the back of my house,
ominous as organ music at a horror show—
hunters eager for pre-autumn kills.

Then, stillness returns for the moment,
but not in my heart that beats
anticipatory grief like pebbles
cannoned into a dark well.

Parable I

By Lopa Banerjee

What parable do I compose
In isolation, reeking of bare silence
As the world, between its quietude and explanation
Of the unprecedented pandemic
Trudges along parallel paths of wisdom, understanding,
Becoming and unbecoming?

Or was it not unprecedented, uncalled for
Ringing the deepest bells of truth
As the air around us evoked
The dark forebodings of ancient ancestors,
The endless circles of the poetry and dance
Of life and death, existence and annihilation
That we sang, unbeknownst, between our sermons
And the cloudburst of postmodern songs?

In parables, we break open,
In parables of our shady, pregnant past
Our light of truth shines. We seek
Answers to the sneaky dance of sudden deaths,
Our fugitive lives wax and wane,
Rough edges smoothen
Moored between flesh and ashes.

Parable II

By Lopa Banerjee

Was it again in her elongated dreams that she gasped for breath? There, at the fag end of the dreams, at the shore of her waking self, she sighed, as the boundaries blurred. She picked up the blossoms of her earthen poems, crushed by the lingering stench and pressure of the weather-beaten times.

Outside, frostbitten, the trees shrank, one by one, in darkened streets. Yet another surge of bodies, dead, rumpled by the north wind. They all had gasped for breath, she was told, the desire to live grew stronger, deeper.

She wondered how parables were made, recycled in the mouths of one generation to the next… the grandmothers' tales, lores, their pale, bleeding lips spoke of cholera, typhoid, tuberculosis, the incessant cycles of disaster-prone communities. They all had gasped for breath, she was told, shrank, then obliterated. Such was the narrative of common humans on the sidewalk, with little or no affiliation. This mammoth wreckage of gasping, dead humans would also go down in history's annals. Or, would history dilute their trails?

It would rain, rain anytime in the asylum now. Clouds would burst forth in a legacy of twisted truths, leaking through cracked walls. All her inmates gasped for breath inside stiffening, dark spaces, 'oxygen' was uncalled for. Was it in this cryptic space between life and death that her mindscape found clarity in the high octave notes of lives resigned?

There was no transit inside the chambers of this subterranean world where inhaling freedom had been imbued with ever-evolving meanings, twirling between the syllables of the self, the microcosm and the macrocosm. Outside, in the bare streets, gunshots resound, screams are born afresh and die out soon, grey, ominous clouds hover in the morning sky with new announcements of death, just a block away. The 'pandemic,' an old utterance now, had stirred and shaken her crust and core a year ago, when she was grasping the language of resistance inside these cracked, creaking walls.

The rickety earth had spilled its leftovers, newer trajectories of survival had reared their heads stronger. Footprints of her old earth still scrawled on her being as she gasped for breath like rhythmic reminders. Yet in between screams and silence, in the desperation of an invisible tomorrow, the desire to live grew stronger, deeper.

Our World Coughs

By Phyllis Becker

It is as if day turned into night in the middle
of the afternoon like a full eclipse.
And now we find ourselves sheltering in place.
Today, the thunder and lightning sound
like the rolling and cracking of huge bowling balls.
It somehow soothes, matches my mood.
I lie in bed and listen, go inward
and back to a time sewing with my mother--
each fabric chosen, pattern pinned, cloth cut through
my eighth-grade anguish. And then with my hair freed
from chemicals, my buoyant 'fro, and the beautiful
clothes I sewed to fit my tall, skinny frame,
I was altered. Now, fifty years later,
my mother alive only in dreams,
I rouse at 5:00 a.m., and I hear
(what I now call) my birds urgently chirping
me out of my waking despair.
Our world coughs, and we have nowhere to run,
nowhere to go, yet it is a new day.
I have bed hair, clothes that fit,
food to eat, savor each breath.

What Goes Around

By Phyllis Becker

I am working hard not to wish this virus on you
because it is wrong, and the virus will do what it does.
I have no control,

even as you risk my life or someone's poor grandma, since you
choose not to cover your mouth and nose.
The irony is you are saved by those you mock.

I have to work even harder not to wish the virus
on you or someone or close to you as an object lesson
because it's that kind of wish that can backfire

and something you might do.
The words and science of respected
men and women don't sway you.

It's you swaying others to listen
to the little devil on their shoulder,
risking thousands.

Oh, how I do not wish
the virus on you or others like you.
I won't risk my peace of mind.

It won't go away with wishes or denial.
You or I can't control it. And did I not hear
that someone close to you got it, someone close to me?
This virus will do what it does.

Ripples

By Smeetha Bhoumik

The euphoria
of high tide
   bursts in ripples on the shore

  Slanted curves.

How the whiteness
     of seashells
is lustrous

   In farewell waves of the setting sun.

Neon glow
of emotions
Lurks beneath the surface

The face is backlit. Unmasked.

   Laughter carries across water.
 Do feelings?

Between grey and ochre
Vast crowds
  Gathered
    On the beach
      Emit emotions
        Not too difficult to read
          Not too difficult to know

We've been there before.

The need to wash away grief
Assuage pain.
Hold hands.
Breathe.
Not sore breaths off four walls
But open rhythmic pulsing beats

Inhale. Exhale. Inhale...exhale...

A vast wind of elaborate texture
Flies over the open sea.

How to Stay Sane When the World Seems Crazy

By Ronda Piszk Broatch

— NYTimes headline, 23 March 2020

Stop and take a breath. The world will keep spinning,

and I remember how I had to lie down after the light
outside the windows left, my fingers frozen to the keyboard
like pigeons in a wind clinging to a building at the end
of a long pier. We wonder *why we catastrophize,*

open the garden shed door after a hard winter to find
our geraniums still green and thriving. Instead of railing
against the shortage of empathy, we *accept uncertainty:*
will it rain today? who will like my post on Facebook,

the photo of my cat resting her chin on the table, or
how a Chinese company sends tens of thousands
of respirator masks to Italy, stapling to shipping crates
lines of Seneca: *We are waves from the same sea, leaves*

from the same tree, and flowers from the same garden.
Today as clouds shelter us like an awning from God, I try hard
to *stick to the facts:* there are sixty-four thousand eighty
four fewer residents of planet earth, that I could say

I love you with two empty soup cans, connected with string.
You would tell me out of one million one hundred eighty-seven
thousand seven hundred ninety-eight cases of coronavirus to *avoid
all-or-nothing thinking.* And I might remind you that in five

minutes of constant rain no one else has died, how I minimized
that link without a second thought. Meanwhile, the world spins,
poverty goes on as it does, and as soon as temperatures rise
I'll put the geraniums outside to drink the downpour,

maybe *get involved* sewing masks for nurses and every
loved one I can put my arms around. You stop and take
a breath, your voice so far away, the scent of soup remaining
strong as you tell me, *take care of yourself.* And I promise I will.

previously published in MiGoZine, 2020

The First Winter

By Wendy Taylor Carlisle

Why do you start out each morning
surprised? Sun in your eyes

as if there would be new news
as if in these days of terror you could

be redeemed by snow
flakes, released and swirling.

It isn't so.

You must crawl forward as usual,
sad patron of the drift.
You must wear these months

around your neck, carry them
on your shoulders.
And still, the cool morning sun,
the dogs sliding on the icy walk.

This Solitude

By Carol Casey

I'm turning into a ghost, not scary, just
unsubstantial as the layers built for/by others
peel off, fade away. This garment's slipping
now, red, ragged, stinky. I look in the mirror
and see not even a vampire's invisibility,
just the ordinary flicker of a fleeting flame.
Some days I feel too old for destiny, or wonder.
All the decrees that chop, shred, divide are
hunting down small birds to trap, taunt, maim.
This forest is full of predators formed from
the contorted mirrors of those who've gained
entrance through the wounds they inflicted.
Every day I must get past them, knowing that
they feed on fear. Each time I walk through,
they dissipate like fog, bide their time.

Over-sanitized, under-washed,
my ragged fragments toss about in each wind.
Eventually, the garment will all blow away.
Time to spin something new, stronger.
Out of what? Some soggy anger matts,
a huge black fear-of-abandonment shroud,
some silver threads of intensity
following their needle of ambition,
a wide expanse of pride, some polyester guilt,
a few colorful yarns of creativity.
Some stained satin sheets of love say,
why make another costume? Now is the time,
when nobody's looking, to work what is.
Keep on sorting, mixing until it makes sense
then sleep on it and see what dreams will come.

*Excerpt from a longer version, first published in Subterranean Blue
Poetry (online journal), 2021. Rights retained.*

Flawless Nature

By Neelam Saxena Chandra

Sitting by a river,
In the hills, I can see
The flawlessness of nature.

How clear is the water of the river
that flows in the valley,
How pure is the air I breathe.
I can feel nature embracing me
As I can't embrace its vastness.
I can only wrap my arms around a tree
That signifies happiness to me.

Why do we destroy the mountains,
green blossoming trees,
and pollute the sparkling rivers?

Is nature reacting in anger
by manifesting diseases and viruses
like COVID—eliminating lives,
For what we humans have done
To the elements of nature?

Two Dead Poets Visit the National Aquarium During the Coronavirus Quarantine

By Liz Chang

They might have come any time—no one would see them—but it is quieter, stiller now. The dead don't worry about surfaces possibly harboring a virus. The dead don't worry about crowds (as they walk through a person, the living may feel a blast of cold air, may look around for a phantom air vent) or tickets. They could have come after hours, but beneath the semi-dark of daytime caustics—pulsing, undulating light—the Blacktip Coral Reef tank is luminous.

Inside the dark amphitheater, beyond a sign marked 'Underwater Viewing Area,' Ralph Angel is perched on the second carpeted stair, his face awash in blue refraction. Descending the last switchback of the Shark Alley ramp, James Schuyler can hear his guttural laugh. *Ah, the joy of the newly dead,* he scoffs. The younger man's levity almost offends him inside this marine cathedral. When at last he sees him, Angel leans back with his right ankle poised on the bulb of his left knee. Even as Schuyler moves closer, there is no rustle of physicality to disturb Ralph's ocean-deep meditation. He briefly looks up as James passes in between him and the glass.

Perhaps as greeting, Angel motions to the tank with a half-open hand, "I think I met that guy last year at AWP!" He gestures to a plump Spotted Unicornfish who flicks a tailfin and darts forward with a singular purpose. It has been almost forty years since Schuyler attended that conference and it was never very crowded. James settles in next to Ralph. They planned to meet here to share in the communion of the tank. They have very little to say to each other, but Ashbury said they should meet and they have nothing if not time.

Someone—not a poet—once said that the ocean floor is less familiar to us than bodies in space. After a few minutes of silence, Schuyler draws in a breath and considers remarking on the school of Garibaldi fish. He's drawn to the deep red of the youngest ones before they turn orange, with their blue-flecked backs. *Impossibly Rothko-red with bits of Porter's sky,* he thinks.

The school of them recall Christmas windows at Barney's in late November. He shivers to think of the cutting wind of Madison Avenue. He can remember cold but safely not feel it. The dead are like the surge and swell of particulates moving under the water's surface, bobbing in the unseen current. It takes effort to stay still like this—for the living, it is the reverse.

Schuyler ruptures the air around them, musing, "Don't you have that line about 'pinpricks of light/opening up a universe without end'? These fish are like that…," he trails off.

For a long moment, Ralph stares at him, almost through him, in a way that might have unnerved Schuyler were he not already a ghost. Then the younger man answers: "'…how such terrible silence/came into the world,'" quoting his companion.

After a breath, Schuyler looks back at Angel, who has settled once again into concentration, reflexively stroking his white soul patch with the side of his thumb. His fist is cupped under his own chin like a mother's hand might reach to tilt up the face of her absentminded son. It is an awkward pose, worn into familiarity over many years. Turning back to the tank, James watches the Reticulated Whiptail Ray glide by, rippling its muscled wings and drawing tiny pebbles up from the sandy bottom as it moves.

There is an echoing sound here, a soft, hollow hum. It sounds like a heart on a stethoscope, and without concurring, the poets know it does not come from either of them. They are dead. The world on the street above is silent, holding its breath.

Too Wide To Bridge

By Kai Coggin

it's good friday,
the middle of the night
and I try to sleep but can't
quiet the mind spinning
in so many directions at once,

it's good friday
and it was good, honestly,
and I didn't even know
the day of the week until I laid down,
spent hours photographing
chipmunks and bluebirds and butterflies
in the spring-bursting sun,

while outside these paradise walls
a covid crucifixion is
hammering nails into boxes holding
thousands of my brothers
and thousands of my sisters,

and tonight
there are prisoners
in hazmat suits
getting paid $6/hr
digging New York mass graves
stacking up pine caskets of the unclaimed,
these are the ones that nobody comes for,
the ones who die alone,
the ones who have no friends or family,
no kids of their own,

and I don't know how to sit with this—
this chasm is too wide to bridge
with a poem,

but it's good friday
and no, no it was not good,
and I just had to write that into the gospel of now.

Outcome

By Candice Louisa Daquin

She came into town
breathless with excitement
they were dying around her
but she wanted to go for coffee
to get her nails done, her hair, wax the city
burn the little temples of obedience
she didn't think a swath of fabric
let alone standing apart like courting
birds
could slow the spread of something
fictional
she was young, though not as young as others thought
Botox took care of that
and a little filler
her heart was set on
kicking up her heels and the virus
was just a news cycle
nothing to take seriously.
Waking in hospital she
momentarily forgot to
smooth her hair down until
she felt her fingers brittle and cracked
her beautiful skin marred with fever
"at least I survived" she smiled
with yellowed teeth, hot with flux
half joking at the scared nurse who
was working her second double shift.
They decided not to tell her yet
until she was out of danger, if indeed she ever
was
that her father, mother and little sister
were not going
to wake up again
and join in her
merriment.

The Day After

By Ed Davis
          For George Floyd

Is that a cardinal I glimpse through glass?
But no—with specs on I see it's a pink
magnolia bloom cupped by the gentle
palm of late April snow.

They predicted an inch, then as much
as three by the time we retired.
I shivered beneath thin covers, wishing
I'd left on the down comforter
I lay beneath all last winter.

Ah comfort!—now there's a word
that describes this unlikely sight:
white on green after relentless grey
of an endless pandemic year.

Hope feels right today following
justice done, as the plague (maybe) fades,
all those hours and days lost to strife
redeemed a little in morning light.

But now sun's gone and snow's gleam
on trees and street is fading fast,
leaving something like peace if not
the full deliverance we crave:
new grass over an old grave.

Phantom Sax Man

By Ed Davis

His sound greets me two blocks away.
Too irregular not to be live, it's *LOUD.*
A busker, I think, though it's only mid-March,
rushing the season in our too touristy town.

I cross the street to avoid several non-
maskers in front of Tom's Market, shielding
my eyes from the setting sun. The music
man has to be at Presbyterian Church,
but so far he is only sound, until

he comes into view at last, standing far back
in the shadows of the portico, wailing away,
using the stone church like a big bowl
from which to send his sweet soul growling

down steps to curl between cars,
halting me in front of Sunrise Café.
Silver-slinky soprano elides to low
bassy rumble hooting up the scale.

My winter-sodden heart gongs in reply.
This phantom saxer isn't playing for money—
no tips to be found in this ghost town today.
And he surely isn't doing it for fame.

Love, then?

As I walk on, his sound fades to a trace.
I recall purple and gold crocuses glimpsed earlier—
like the sax man's song, spring's first breaths
of resurrection following a year of so much death.

Masks, Flowers, Garlic

By Annie Finch

> *Death is also a*
> *Woman who plows the fields*
>
> —Jennifer Goldwasser

Hands are washed, breath held; a wedding band
Is twisted; someone's voice will carry, low,
Then find itself, at last, alone and slow
With the unfinished. What is left to plan?

She shakes the silence that has locked us so
With steady Feet. The truths of Her demands,
Like birds' songs, carry far more than we'd planned
They ever would above the traffic flow.

So we sing and clean, reach out as best we can,
Plowing our days towards mercy or the blow;
Masks, flowers, garlic, will be ours to show
When She who's come to stalk with opened hands,

Whispering "hold it close" or "let it go,"
Unfurls the reaping there is left to sow.

Grateful in the Time of COVID

By Linda McCauley Freeman

I am grateful for the pause,
the time we have wanted all our adult lives
for nowhere to go, nothing pressing to do. I am
grateful for the organized closets and all my books,
finally shelved alphabetically by author and
categorized. And for the time to read them.

I am grateful for the decades of poems
transferred from scraps of paper, now edited
and filed on my computer, ready for submission.
I am grateful for the many poems accepted already.
Maybe this will be next?

I am grateful for returning to cloth napkins
and leisurely dinners with wine, with my husband,
with no crushing stress for either of us to be anywhere
else but here, with each other, fully. I am so grateful
for the pause, the hamster wheel running wild
forced still and silent, creating the possibilities
inherent in just being.

(Previously published online in the Journal of Expressive Writing Blog)

Confetti Of Aftermath

By Linda McCauley Freeman

No celebration rains from rooftops
for our solitary parade. We are not
victors, not heroes, but survivors.
This pandemic holding us hostage,
away from one another, our normal lives,
until disconnection is normal,
becomes who we are, alone
with the self we have avoided.

Is that then heroism?
To face oneself every day with no buffer,
no illusion? No reason for makeup,
showers or even changing clothes.

To stop the doingness and busy-ness,
the excuses for our not beingness.
Perhaps not being
was its own solitary confinement.

Now enforced, we may find out
who we are, what we want,
so when we step back
into the world, the welcome will leave
us hoarse with shouting
as confetti rains on our solitary parade.

Duplex

By Kelsey Goeres

I'm normally a friendly neighbor — especially by Los Angeles' standards. But when we moved into this Duplex on Orange St. at the beginning of the pandemic, I never said hello to the people living in the other half of this house. Sometimes I see them, a couple around our age — early 30s — coming home from a grocery run, walking their dog. The dog they call Mama, who lies in their tomato plants when they're not home. I avoid eye contact like a shy child on her first day of school, in a way that is inconsistent with my personality. But this hasn't been a normal year, and this hasn't been a normal home. More of a cross between a bunker and a secret garden. When we do accidentally cross paths, I wonder: Can you hear my primal cries, regular as a rooster? My panic attacks that shake our walls like earthquakes — do they shake yours, too? Can you hear us fighting about which activities are safe, defensive and stubborn as cats? Can you hear us laugh at old shitty movies like hyenas who just escaped from the zoo? Sometimes I hear you sing classic rock when you vacuum. It is almost too much for me to bear. You're trying your best over there just like us, aren't you? I never said hello, but I know you want a new job. I hear you in meetings, working from home. You're so patient and smart. I can tell you want to help people. I hear your partner tell you it wouldn't hurt to follow-up after that interview. I can tell you're nervous about it, but he's right, it wouldn't hurt. I can hear your exercise bike, your need to move like a hamster in a cage. I can hear your voice change when you call your mother, how it becomes softer when you switch to Spanish.

I have felt so far away this year, on an island. We share the island with two other people, a line in the sand, a row of palm trees that blocks the pairs from seeing each other. We can hear whisperings of life on the other side, repetitions from parrots who fly freely between both camps, and sometimes that's enough to keep from walking into the ocean. It was just enough.

Be Still, Listen

By Amata Natasha Goldie

Be still
Listen

The serenity of the natural world beckons,
There are no planes in the sky now
Only birds,
And clouds, painted with Gods paintbrush

The cities and the townships have quietened,
The pollution has lifted from great Gaia
For a century her breath has laboured
And now humanity wears the mask
To protect us
From a virus of our own making

Be still
Listen

Her medicinal treasures are fecund
She grows the cures for all ailments
She still bleeds oil to fuel our machines
And the almighty Sun gives so abundantly of his free energy
But still, we don't listen

An agenda devised an eon ago,
And a virus patented a year ago
Now takes centre stage
In the drama play
Another test
Between two opposites
Made famous in Hollywood scripts

Be still
Listen

Humanity stayed home,
And accepted
Fear reigned supreme
And survival became paramount

Some prayed and connected,
Others lost themselves in despair
Acts of kindness
And acts of war,
The choice lay within

Question what you hear
Question what you believe
The unveiling is ripe,
For those who yearn to see,
Empty your mind
And bathe your soul
In the miracle of the natural world

She does not seek to control us, to surveil us, or to vaccinate us
There are no patents on sovereignty and freedom
There is no darkness in the natural world
Even in the depths of caves shine crystalline light,
Just as stars sparkle in the midnight sky
Yet the agenda of darkness
Is ever-present upon Her
And the battle is hidden from our view

Be still
Awaken

Letter to My Future Self

By Marci Hannewald

Dear Future Self:

You will remember this day.

You'll recall, like it was yesterday, the glorious robin's egg blue skies, soaking up spring's sweet sunshine peeking through fluffy cottontail puffs from behind the barely budding dogwoods and determined maples. You'll hear the birdsong pierce the crisp morning air like an Easter hymn and feel the earth loamy and damp under your bare toes after last night's hard rain. You'll fill your lungs with a calming infusion of nature at her finest, joyful and fresh with the promise of a new season, and inhale deep appreciation for these tiny miracles after a long, gray Michigan winter.

You'll exhale, and you'll know, as I do now, that everything you need is in this present moment.

You'll remember the storms and the uncertainty of this age, when a pandemic gripped the world with its spiny, brutal teeth and life as we knew it ground to a halt. You'll be reminded of working from home, with its paradox of endless conference calls and strangely empty solitude, so gratified for your employment in a period of crisis. You'll look back on the days when both the big box stores and your local businesses closed, one by one, by government order, until only the essentials remained open for groceries and gas and medicine and the like, and you tried to push away worries about what might come next.

You'll shake your head, reliving the week when toilet paper became the community's most sought-after commodity and your neighbors ducked their heads and looked away instead of saying hello in the aisles of Kroger. You'll feel compassion for the way you tried mightily to distract yourself from unproductive hamster wheel thinking through mindless TV and internet surfing, cooking, cleaning, and stress eating.

You'll be forever grateful to Carter for his daily online livestream yoga classes, for hilly riverside hikes, for phone and Skype calls with the people you love most, and for the steady companionship of your sweet senior dog who's been there for you, unfailingly, each day for the past 11 years.

You'll remember it all, every bit, as clear and real and true as when it first unfolded. You'll be reminded of your own inner fortitude and your ability to keep going even in the tough times while seeing the good in every situation. You'll know that you survived heartbreak, despair, and fear of the unknown before and came out stronger and wiser on the other side, and you'll feel comforted in the knowledge that you can – and you will – do it again. And again and again, dodging and weaving amidst whatever curveballs this rollicking planet throws at you because you're resilient and stubborn and hopeful, and you know there's learning to be found in every experience, no matter how challenging.

Today's lesson, like so many others, is to pause, come to the center, and give thanks for what's right here, right now. Your mission is to discover that this too shall pass, just as sure and fleeting as the endless cloudscapes in the bright spring sky. You've been gifted this day as a reminder that all is well, even when you can't yet see through to the other side.

Breathe in. Breathe out. Remember. Say it again. Everything you need is in this present moment.

You've got this.

A Virus Plagued Night

By Sarita Jenamani

This nocturnal solitude
makes us mourn the moment given
the images of those handwritten notes,
family heirlooms,
and poems sent in the hope
they would get buried
alongside those who die
in hospitals alone

How can we forget
contours of those
who could not caress
cheeks of their dear departed
one last time holding their hands
and seeing them dying gracefully

We will be alive
to what happens
before the breadth diffuses
in the shadow of night
and the dream dissolves

But we know
a little harbor lies in the sand
of our grieve-stricken survival
that builds a boat
out of this temporal wrack
enabling us sail towards a new dawn

Spring 2020

By Sarita Jenamani

This spring
a dark sign looms
in the far-east horizon
Silk route brings us
neither softness of silk
nor aphrodisia of spices
myriad of dawns
the vermilion silhouette of night
rises to mark the mirror of death.

This spring
denies dignity
to the dead
turn prayers into torture
as the honeycomb of memory
stacks the images of dead ones

This spring
When I write, I write
only silence and solitude
by a flickering of hope
while attempting to overcome the dark

Gaia's Hammer

By David Kann

We were neck deep in the Big Muddy
And the big fool said to push on.
                    Pete Seeger

Gaia's rage, her forge, is blazing
white hot and flickering blue flames.
Her hammer hovers
over our lost, stupid selves
sprawled on her anvil
to be pounded into an apter form.

There was a time we breathed with her lungs
and her breath filled us,
and her whole dappled world
lived in our sight,
and our sight lived in her eyes.
The ocean's hiss and crash,
birdsongs' echo in the trees
the crackle of corn growing in the night,
pines booming in the wind--
all lived in our ears' soft coils,
and all our hearing was her voice.
We contained her, filled with her joy
as she contained us, swaddled in her ecstasy.
Our thoughts were her passions
and when she moved within us,
we knew the reason of our passion.
Her mothering hands cradled us
at that shimmering point where past and present meet.
Her spirit sang in our bodies' bliss
and our bodies' motions spoke her will.

She's been loving and patient,
hoping our ignorance was our youth--
selfish as newborns who live
out their almighty madness
of owning the teat, perpetually offered,
so we crane our necks, whining,
lips forever puckered,

crazy to suckle no matter the cost.
Unable to compute the cost;
impossible to imagine a cost;
unwilling to pay the cost,
self-driven further and further
into the quicksand muck of our greed,
sinking deeper with each step
to suffocate--mouths, noses, ears and eyes
filled with our own strewn, stinking shit--
prophets dishonored;
reason disregarded.
Now we listen to frauds
who look to power for truth
and not to the skin of the earth
to find it in bark beetles' script
or in the coded flash of lightning bugs.

She's endured us enough.
She's enlisted her other children
to demolish us with the diseases of our gluttony:
Cattle. Bats. Pangolins. Snakes, Monkeys.
Mad Cow Disease, Covid-19. Ebola, AIDS, SARS, MERS,
and all our appetites' debts have come due:
killing heat, lethal cold,
drought that withers wheat and corn,
leafless thickets where children huddle, too thirsty for tears,
arms and legs like sticks, swollen bellies,
populations wandering across wastelands
where dust rises in brown clouds under a red sun
tsunamis rise engorged like gluttonous flesh,
carrying swollen, stinking bodies floating,
slowly spinning seaward
in retreating tides, black with sewage.

How to cure a lethal disease?
Poison it, burn it, freeze it,
drown it, starve it, crush it;
turn life against it.
Free the organism of the fatal blight.

World Without Us

By Alfred LaMotte

Written during the Covid-19 pandemic of 2020

I'm sorry to say how sonorous earth would be
without us, how clear the voice of streams
plucking their harps of stone,
the waterfall-leaping salmon chant,
goat bleats erupting from the torn
pomegranate of the nanny.
How fresh the smell of rain and sweet
the pollen on the bee's feet, hum
of rummaging among wild roses:
but who would make the Poem?
A dolphin perhaps, or an elephant on the shore,
susurrus of black flies fleeing her swished ear?
A stir in the leaf-languid jasmine, rattle
of palm fronds scenting storm, frolic
of pelicans skimming whitecaps for carp?
A verse of the Poem might be
a logos of waves stroking coral, pink
in the grouper's gaze, his mouth articulating
bubbles in the mindfulness of the shark.
Another, the whirring return of vast hunger
to the belly of the hummingbird. Or rustle
in the pelt of an elk before his bugling stuns
the world back into silence.
How patiently the stars would listen
above the basso continuo of microbes
intoning their restless intuitions.
But who would hear the night itself
and give voice to quietness?
Perhaps the owl, that darkling huntress
zeroing down on her mouse…
Oh the Poem will survive us, surely,
other tongues enunciate the descant
of the blood, wingéd and four-leggéd singers,
free to be their savage selves as we
once were, but humbler, quieter, knowing
beyond knowledge when to stop.

Social Distance

By Alfred LaMotte

Written during the Covid-19 pandemic of 2020

I'm cracking

Masked like a robber, I went to the grocery store just for
chocolate peanut butter Haagen-Dazs.

I can't wash my hands any more, they're raw.

The hallelujah chorus of Spring peepers rejoicing in the wetlands
is the only good news.

Last week my Rx was ginger root, lemon juice, and turmeric;
this week, ginger root, lemon juice, and Merlot.

The sting of Clorox is the new normal.

I am haunted by guilt because I may have too much toilet paper.

But a sweetness, perhaps the taste of justice, pervades every atom of
my body, even where it hurts.

I walk my dog through pools of daffodils in the silent, abandoned
park, thinking of my weary daughter, and a million other valiant
health care workers, going to her job each morning with no face
cover, no distance, no dream.

Maybe this life is not true-or-false; maybe it's a multiple choice quiz.

(a) Things are better than they feel.

(b) Things are worse than they feel.

(c) I contribute to human civilization by giving a $40 tip to the pizza
delivery man.

(d) Just as I fall asleep, I see our nation drowning in a golden tidal
wave of compassion, the bodies of Donald Trump and Nancy Pelosi
bobbing gently, arms entwined, on the clear waters of April, dolphins
exploring ancient canals among ruined towers draped in honeysuckle,
the dome of Congress changed into a giant hummingbird feeder.

(e) Tears, and more tears.

(f) All of the above.

Two Weeks After My Second Moderna Shot

By Andrea Livingston

On my evening walk, a high-pitched sound swirls through
the pines, as if a windstorm were electrifying bare branches,

as if their cones were clacking together like castanets.
But there is no wind tonight, only the bizarre buzz in the air.

Could it be the roar of my neighbor's lawnmower?
No, the shrill notes are falling from the highest limbs.

Years ago, I heard a similar ruckus at a Day of the Dead
celebration. A couple were shaking their maracas

so vigorously, I feared their rattles would break, the beans
spill all over the street. But when they varied the rhythm,

tapping the instruments lightly with their fingertips,
the vibrations rose into the night like hummingbird wings.

I read billions of cicadas are returning to the East Coast
after 17 years underground where they've been busy

digging tunnels, drinking sap from tree roots, preparing
to surface into sunlight to sing their seductive songs.

Perhaps some have already decided to migrate to California
and sprout like crocuses from our fertile spring soil.

Walking down the wooded path, I've taken this long, silent year,
I imagine hearing their come-hither calls, reminding me it's safe

to inhale the evening air without fear of the blue-black vulture above.
I've learned there's a time for silence, a time for song.

(Published in May 2021 in the online journal *Global Poemic: Kindred
Voices in the Era of COVID-19*)

This morning: July 6, 2020

By Andrea Livingston

my Instacart order arrived:
three pounds of ripe tomatoes,
though I ordered only three,
a 24-pack of Crystal Geyser Spring water,
in case the virus swims in the tap, too.

Before freezing, I disinfect boxes
of pad Thai, red curry rice,
gluten-free pizza with a Clorox wipe.
Then, use another to kill any microbe
alive on the plastic bag of organic broccoli.

I worry all this time disinfecting
might interfere with other plans:
my online strength training,
FaceTime with my sister,
Zoom dinner party with friends.

While I scrub my hands
with antibacterial soap
for as long as it takes to sing
Happy Birthday twice,
a woman in Sub-Saharan Africa
walks up a steep unpaved road
to the public water spigot.

She hopes she will be lucky today:
be able to fill her large jug
with water barely blue and clear
as spring rain, enough
to quench her baby's thirst
throughout the dry, windy night.

She does not mind
the jug's heaviness on her head,
the burn of the red clay
between her toes.
Nor does she know
the name of the newest plague.

She has no time
to worry about such things.

Orange

By John C. Mannone

In my dream, I kissed you under the clementine sky
of Titan, that cream-sickle orange moon of Saturn.
After last night's storm of methane rain, I didn't
see a rainbow. The low angled sun filtered too much.
It's as if all the colors melted into orange—
        I wonder if that is the color of hope for us.

When I awakened, the scent of limonene in the air
amidst the petrichor in the orchard, I learned
of the tornadic thunderstorm, the devastation
in the river valley, and of the aftermath of arguments.

When I smell orange peel, I think of my mother
at the charcoal grill, placing the dried skin of a Florida
orange to entice the appetite for what's to come
while warding off the pesky yellow jackets, she knew
how to calm a swarm or chase the storm away.

My father, too. I didn't know it then, but when he
fought with my mother with acidic words, he'd grab
a navel orange and a loaf of Moranto's bread and share
it with me, wedge after wedge, a yearning in his eyes.

They'd find some sweetness mixed with the bitter,
just like the kumquat words full of golden orange
syllables to sing in between their kisses.

Often enough, I'd find a sweet orange in my lunch box
together with a breaded chicken cutlet sandwich and
other memories in the quiet time of my later years, like
vanilla ice cream and canned fruits with little mandarin
oranges, and a shot of dry red wine, something
my mother loved, and loved to make.

There's always a pomelo's pale yellow light to intoxicate
the skies with the taste of freedom, not only of that moon
a late-rising gibbous waning at zenith on April 19, 1775,
it was full, anxious in the coming dawn of revolution.

But in this century, our bodies are fighting their own
revolution. The spiked enemy, orange in the light
of a scanning electron microscope, threatens not just
the body. Right now

my neck cranes toward the heavens, my heart red
as saffron, yellow as its crocus flower, and orange
                    as my hope is for us.

* The orange is a hybrid between pomelo (*Citrus maxima*) and mandarin
(*Citrus reticulata*)

Rue

By Jennifer Martelli

And then I realized the coronavirus was a woman

who's been ignored for too long, and now

she holds sway, she lumbers like

the Elephant Queen, the big tusker,

the last of her kind, determined to end

wherever she wants.

No one dares

bump into this woman. She puts on her red

pearl crown and everybody—are you

happy now—has to watch her, listen

to what she has to say.

I told my friends this today,

some virtually, some six feet away. I told them this

through the dry and cold ides of March air and,

maybe because they love me, no one looked surprised.

Offering Through the Fence

By Jennifer Martelli

When my neighbors brought home their newborn girl,

we could only speak through those diamond-spaces of the lattice.

They held the baby up, and I bobbed my head to see her and admire.

During that last trimester, they'd left their cherry tomatoes to grow

wild and offered me all that reached through the fence and dangled

    like weighty X-mas bulbs into my yard.

Today, the last Saturday of this infected summer,

I bring our old toaster, the one whose coils won't get hot,

to the trash bin filled with things my kids left behind:

Mia's gold wristlet from some prom, an odd Nike sneaker deep beneath

Michael's bed, stacks of their spiral notebooks I don't dare read.

I hear the baby's cries clearly though, in the late summer dusk.

The tomatoes glow red and beckon me: they are so ripe,

they drop all thin-skinned near bursting into my open palm.

Hallowed be My Name

By Kate Maxwell

It's been months since I saw my mother.
Her lilting voice, repeated platitudes ooze
warm syrup in my ear: sweet, sticky tones

trickling down the line to clad the cracks
and channels of forgotten days. Her rusty
laugh, my name held in her mouth, as the

softest prayer. Such sacred love, taken for
granted, like breath, the unbroken beating
of my heart, and sometimes I cannot even

make the call for fear that her loneliness
will sliver beneath skin, burrowing deep
inside me for days. Easier to cover time in

dull endless tasks, deny the ache each time
I hear the cracking in her voice, the whistle
of an icy wind whipping at her solitude.

A carer brings her tea and a biscuit to warm
the chill of her children's long absence.
I summon up her crinkled smile as she cries

'Oh, I've just been brought a lovely cup of tea,'
as if this will compensate for what we've done
to her, left her alone, now we're too busy for

the quaint hum of old love. And we will claim
this callous pandemic as the palisade that keeps
us apart, but I know. I know your golden child

would rather bleed into the inky indulgence of all
those carefully placed words than have to suffer
the clear, searching gaze of her beloved hazel eyes.

A Psalm of Hope

By Kavita Ezekiel Mendonca

Blessed are you if the breath of life
Has chosen you for a new day
Allowed you to waken early
With eyes to see the early skies of a new dawn,
If you rise late, to behold the bright yellow sun.
Blessed are you who have been granted ears to hear
The sweet symphony of birds, the gentle sound of trees
Whisper in the morning breeze outside the kitchen window.

Blessed are you if with nostrils filled with breath
To smell the aroma of ginger tea or steaming coffee,
 If in a place called home the breath of life
Filled you like an overflowing water pot
Drawn from the village well,
You have awakened to the gift of hope.

The world will look different if you can spend a day
Without fearful utterances of the words
Virus, Pandemic, Lockdown,
Render them voiceless and faceless
Even for a moment to grasp the gift of time.

From a new morning until
The splendid moon pours moonlight
Makes its announcement of night,
You have lived a day of hope, your prayers
For those robbed of life's breath
Will bring to your consciousness
The precious gift of life granted to you.

The world will be restored to its natural order
In God's good timing with hope around every corner
Reach out your arms, commune with it
Breathe hope and pass it on.

When The World Ends

By Richard Modiano

White dust will fill the air like
the curtain at the end of a play.
A rain of desperate bodies will fall from the windows
of burning buildings, drumming the concrete below.
Men with splinters in their eyes
will stumble through the streets choked with debris;
women clutching babies
will pick through the rubble and tear out their hair.
Our generation will go to its grave shouting its
last words into a cell phone.
Or perhaps it will arrive as a thief in the night,
step by invisible step. Factories
will disappear overseas, and corporations
vanish into thin air, taking jobs and retirement funds with them.
Cities dying from the inside out will spread like ringworm,
the shrapnel spray of suburbs slicing through forest and field.
Wars will reach from continent to continent and neighborhood to
neighborhood –
the terrorists won't make peace with the horrorists
who would enforce it at any price,
who keep trying to impose harmony between oppressed and
oppressor with fear and firepower.
Gas prices will rise with global temperatures and tides,
acid rains will fall with the last of the redwoods,
computer systems crash with stocks and stock markets…
A virus spreading from an outdoor market
from spittle carried on the air that blankets the globe,
until one day *everyone* has COVID –
Or else the pandemic will abate,
business will continue as usual:
prison guards pace concrete tombs,
psychiatrists contemplate madness,
demons glare from the eyes of ministers,
consumers bought and sold in the marketplace.
It's after the end of the world, whispers the homeless man,
don't you know that yet?
Others, mysterious and knowing,
who have held themselves aloof from the discussion
until now, finally interject: "*Which* world?"

Let's Continue

By Antoni Ooto

no matter how much rain falls
you will be all right

recall nature
waking a waiting field

where all hopes soak
nudging a belief in renewal

like a monk dropping seed
faithfully keeping that noble vow
blessing its fairness
leaning forward in peace, sowing trust

Today When I Can Do Nothing

By Nynke Salverda Passi

I hug our maple as if it were the body
of the man I love, who is not here

but an ocean away, perhaps sipping wine
on his patio on a hot spring evening,

watching the lit eye of the half-blind moon.
The bark feels shaggy under my fingers,

rhytidome of narrow longitudinal fissures
deepening into gray ruffled ridges,

formation of multiple layers of suberized
periderm, cortical and phloem.

Green leaf-lungs breathe above me,
shivering with wind the way my alveoli expand

under my coat, inside my flesh—
on a loop, from my first conscious breath

in the morning when I rise from dream
till evening when I dream again.

Everyone knows that trees are the lungs
of the earth. The lungs of the earth

burn in Australia, Oregon, California,
but we humans pay little attention.

Now people's lungs in hospital beds fill
with fluid, drowning us from the inside.

A virus invades, pushing out air.
A virus invisible to the naked eye

brings to its knees the world economy.
Clouds still travel overhead without keeping

social distance, their voluptuous bodies
tightly pressed together, but I can go

nowhere. I sit on the back steps and drink
tea from a chipped cup, listening

to the soft chants of the chimes,
the rustle of leaves, the whispering wind.

Then I walk around our still snowy yard
where the first frail green sepals

of rosebuds sprout, where catfish glide
under the cellophane liquid surface

of Louden pond no longer stiffened
with ice. I whisper into the crowns

of the maple, the birch, the oak,
and place my palms softly

on familiar bark, letting each
tree know I will do better,

helping it breathe,
helping it live.

A Lesson in Empathy: A Cento

By Nynke Salverda Passi

The Barcelona opera house,
the *Gran Teatre del Liceu*, resumes

its theatrical season with a concert
attended by 2,292 potted plants.

The plants, raised in nurseries across the city,
are all lushly, fancifully dressed in green.

A string quartet named UcaLi delivers
an eight-minute rendition of Giacomo Puccini's

Crisantemi. The musicians bow
to the leafy audience. "Nature reclaims spaces

humans took for granted," artist Eugenio Ampudia
explains. He adds, "The performance extends

the concept of empathy to other species,
striking new balance." In the background plays

on a loop a susurration of wind whistling
through trees, which serves as a plant applause.

The language of music is supposed to tell
the plants what humans have endured

in these past three months of quarantine:
how confined human lives have been, how hard

it is to live within four tight walls, forced
to be idle—patient, lonely, waiting.

The 2,292 plants in their tight ceramic pots
sit still and listen. Like they always do.

War Unconquered by the Pandemic

By Suman Pokhrel

Translated from Nepali by Abhi Subedi

The walk
about to begin
was stopped.
The meeting about to happen,
was halted.
The regular rhythms of life
were deferred.

All the hastes
deemed vital
slipped out, fell,
and got entangled.

The hugs pined were tossed,
desperately, in secluded spaces,
the normal cycle of human karma
turned chaotic.

But the march of
the high spirit did not stop.
The rays of hope
continued to shine.
The windows and doors
of the myriad alternatives
did not go into slumber.

Scenes and colours
might have changed,
the walks and paths
might have been blocked,
but the perpetual movement of life
did not stop and went on.

Wind on the Face

By Mario Rigli

In our alleys,
and blood running through our arteries,
fear flutters and grins
leaving us fatigued on the ground
in silence, without choice,
away from our loved ones
with no voice to cry out to God.
This cannot be the fate of humans.
The wind on the face feels like
the flapping of wings,
of a dragon or a plague bat.

Where Faith Floats

By Jeannie E. Roberts

whisker-like barbels
covid corona stones
flowers fade

petals droop
midst the watery drop of decay
the pandemic persists

has lengthened its stay
yet faith floats
it streams within being

breathes amid bones
rises from understory
sips from robust shores

where mother soil
nurtures her stems
as marsh marigold

dips her rooted legs
absorbs the theriac of Earth
here well-being brims

with humanity's hope
and the bristled foes sink
where the virus dissolves

swimming in healing waters
Devī the divine feminine
cradles the stoned
mourns the swallowed
blesses the ones who've drowned

OHM

By Cheran

Translated from Tamil by Anushiya Ramaswamy

This is I
softer than a jasmine flower
prohibited from adorning hair
of the gods

This world was created by my thousands of dreams
when I was the forests, trees, mountains,
and birds.

All destroyed by human footfalls

Today
the howl that burst
out of me
from the great contagion
sorrow and suffering:
"Ohm."

Then,
unable to bear
the torture
my testimony
to the soldiers
was also
"Ohm."

That and everything
Has no magical power.

Dreams, These Days

By Nandini Sahu

Dreams, these days, are of the
moon and moon-manufacturer!
The gripe translucent skies in the night
the mood swings of solitude, the cognizance of the air, purer,
the memories of missing moon motif, a vanished delight.

Dreams, these days, are of the sea and the seafarer.
The uncluttered, sweeping ocean
epitomizes much more
than an unbiassed body of water;
it embodies a malicious elegance
that never hesitates to induce the narrator.

Dreams, these days, are of some
make-believe love and some eternal lover.
Ahh! Genuine love is measured by how deep you tumble
and adjudicated; mediated by how trivial you are,
how willing to scuttle
just to save it and make it linger.

Dreams, these days, are of a
comrade and about some paramour.
It is resolute by how keen you are to unclutter.
Offer your conviction. It is generous, incredible
and apparently very kind.
It is, of course, often biased, it is colour blind.

Dreams, these days, are of travel and the traveler.
The wanderer and the wanderlust,
the reminiscence and rumination.
Do not foldaway lost travel stories to the hermit's harbour
there is a great lot you ought to see post contagion.

Dreams, these days are of many lands,
many homes and the homemaker.
There is boundless share your passion
daily does sought to travel.
You need to unpack right away, keep your luggage at bay.
You are not parting, your authority
shall you take back, oh seafarer!
Dreams these days are of a long life—

glorious, happier, healthier, better.
Still, if you succumb, the show goes on
even minus you, so don't despair.
Dream anyway, love anyway;
you shall soon find your 'home' awfully closer!
The marvels of the mourned sound colossal;
they may, as well, entice and lure.

A Parody of Love

By Nandini Sahu

A parody of love with my love today, about a lampoon.
A caricature of pseudo-love to laugh
with my true-love, a burlesque.
That's the fun mood today about this conformist,
ahh his WhatsApp status -- *'the guardian of ancient civilization!'*

What pompous was he when he met me online
over a lecture I delivered on Culture Studies.
He pretended and pretended to be a part of whatever
I said and did; he called himself
even my personal, singular guardian!

He decided that I fell in love with him,
as he was so irresistible!
He thought he was most welcome on my vestibule.
Words of flattery galore, and sycophancy was his syllable.
He simply ordered me to be agreeable
admirable and amicable.

When I said, "I don't know you, who the hell are you?"
he declared that I was only a shy woman,
I was not at all disagreeable.
After all, the ornament of a modest woman is being amiable.
He called me, sent mails;
he pretended that my silence was affable.

Love, you are so funny, you created
an innovative narrative out of it,
'Love in the Time of Covid' when he offered me gift packets of
Remdesivir, steroids, plasma, Tocilizumab and Favipiravir.
He hated my disinterestedness
in his gifts and bouquets of flower.

He declared via emails that he looked great with biceps
which I cannot but admire -- in fact
any woman would fall for him.
I didn't pay any heed, he was furious, he demanded--
I would look conspicuous
only if we walk together, composed.

How could he have liked that a woman, a mere woman,
didn't value his love, his generosity
and his acceptance? He belongs a to 'School of Thought'
where women are Goddesses, Mother-Deities,
but not normal respectable creatures.

He believed in the shameless privileges
and primacies of the rich.
I could do nothing to erase the feudal mindset.
He stood for hours in front of my house, he was sure
one day I would respond
and submit to him, without a doubt.

He used click-baits in his emails, and thumbnail links,
specially designed to catch my attention and to entice me.
He tempted me with promises of awards,
as if I looked for those! Deceptive, sensationalized,
misleading stuff he sent in profusely.

Love you don't belong to this world,
it's a foul world of hegemony.
You believe in reverence for a woman
here and now, not just in the femme idol in a temple.
You wish to punish this man of false agony.
I assure you, fools are better ignored,
for them you can't create an ebony.

A Poor Person's Precarious Pace And Spaces

By Ndaba Sibanda

Her efforts to hold back, to hold herself
Against hurtling and hurting helplessly
With a hungry, tiny child strapped to her back
Are a betrayal, as she bursts into tears and fury
Her hiding husband betrayed her, battered her
She is on the brink of soundness. She is shaky
Hoping to ward off hunger and helplessness
Famine weighs on her fragile body, her mind
As she takes precarious steps that are oblivious
To the world of lockdowns and social distancing
She is dead, deaf, defenceless against a new reality
Ushered in by an eerie, unseen virus, she wobbles on

Fourth Wave

By Ram Krishna Singh

I don't recognise
the bright new star in the sky:
a beacon of hope
they say a new age begins
on earth the virus mutates

scaring millions
post-Christmas repeat events
no vaccination
could change astro-calendar
of universal revenge

remains of prayer
now wrapped in gift box, held up
shipping delays
no burial, no third day
total lockdown, here and there

At the Sound of Tsuzumi

By Kalpna Singh-Chitnis

Behind the masks are eyebrows,
cheekbones and jawlines.
The faces have disappeared.

The one who has stolen all faces has no face.
Or maybe it does, 6.18 million and counting.
Stretched up to the horizon in the arena—

it appears on the stage like a Kabuki performer
and disappears with a generation
stuffed in its Kimono.

It is the dance of the century.
The sky is a drum
beating all night.

We slip on the mask of the moon
and dance alone and together.
We learn the steps unlearned.

At the curious sounds of *Tsuzumi*
we rise breathing deeply,
and breathless, we fall.

The Poet is Gone

By Kalpna Singh-Chitnis

The poet is gone. The poet is gone, leaving a chest behind.

In the chest, there are a thousand letters to a dictator,
hundreds to his own followers, and one to himself about his
dream of becoming a singer, and someday living on farmland.

His being as a poet was accidental.
The burden of earning bread and butter
had dragged him to the city from his mountain abode.

From the capital's streets to the bulletin room,
he covered every piece of news and more.
He was worried about pollution and the virus,

that could kill the masses of nations in droves. In his worries,
he forgot all about his dreams. And as he sipped his last drink
and made one last ring of smoke sitting at his writing-table,

he realized it was too late. His organs gave up.
His lungs collapsed. Tied in a hospital bed all alone,
he wanted to sing but couldn't. He tried to write a note but failed.

The poems he wrote were timbers from the mountains,
fired up with his spirit. The flame he ignited lit many candles
and consumed his dreams.

The poet is gone. The poet is gone, leaving a legend behind.

O, Captain!

—After Walt Whitman

By Kalpna Singh-Chitnis

You cannot blame it all on June gloom,
sitting in your living room, surfing channels
watching plague, politics, and war.

I turn the TV off and read Whitman—
"O, Captain! my Captain!..."
"O the bleeding drops of red..."

I can't wait for the sun to arrive in the eastern hemisphere.
The night sails like a mammoth ship in dark rivers, scooping the dead.
My father, mother, sister, and brother are ailing. Friends have left too soon.

Hark! I hear the faint moaning of the cities shackled from afar.
The buildings hang from the sky lifeless, their tongues out the windows.
The doors are closed, but the oxygen has escaped.

There aren't enough shrouds and wood left in the market.
Like doctors, nurses and essential staff, the forests working
around the clock are making oxygen, coffins, and kindle for cremation.

The animals on the graves appear orphaned. Their masters have left.
The banyan trees stand humble in the country carrying clay pots
hanging from their necks, like the *Bhistis* offering water

to the thirsty souls wandering in the state of *Bardo.*
Shiva roams with his third eye open
in villages and towns and charnel grounds,

emitting fire from the center of his brows,
lighting pyres of the abandoned on river beds,
drinking toxins, flowing in the water to purify the rivers.

Covered in ashes amidst the embers flying,
he contains the spread. He does not exhale.
He is blue, turning darker blue.

The Himalayas melt in grief.
The Ganges widens her shores.
There are more pyres on the ground tonight than stars lit in the sky.

The truth sounds like a lie. But it isn't.
There aren't enough beds and oxygen in the hospitals.
There aren't enough vaccines and medical supplies.

Who is accountable? Who is accountable?
Who is accountable? I beg for help—
help the helpless!

Friends, who couldn't come forward have promised,
they will forward my plea to the rich *NRIs*.
A slap, right in my face!

For the first time, I'm angry
for not being wealthy enough like Gates,
to help my country breathe with one fat check.

Why do I worry? Thirty-three million gods will take care of everything.
Why do I bother? 1.36 billion people will manage their country.
O sister, you will be okay. O Mother, try to sleep now.

I shall breathe for you with my lungs expanded to the continents.
Hope isn't a luxury, it is a necessity.
I invite the *Bell* and sit in silence.

I write an alphabet on a piece of paper and repeat,
until it burns a hole in my heart.
O for Oxygen, O for Oxygen, O for Oxygen.

"O, Captain! my Captain! rise up and hear the bells."

A poem in the wake of the deadly second wave of COVID-19

**Bardo – A transitional state between death and rebirth. *Shiva – A Hindu deity of Annihilation and Purification. *NRIs - Non-Resident Indians. *Bhistis – A tribe of traditional water bearers in India and Pakistan. *Bell – Meditation Bell*

Sanctified

By Donna Snyder

She can make the heat death of the universe
a thing of beauty,
and an exploding star, an object of desire.
But the gravity
of untimely death eludes her magic. Killers
proceed like a curse
written in an ancient alphabet. Death,
indifferent to color or class,
turns crowns of glory into meat hooks,
pierces our flesh, steals
our breath, pulls us into the final black hole.
Our bodies, sanctified,
the mix of every color together, disappear
into the ultimate dark.

Insane "New" Normal

By Megha Sood

Like a blind cave
brittle rib cage hosting the infection
an unwanted guest:
the virus opens its mouth
its glistening black teeth
in the dead of the night

devours everything
precious and beautiful
cleaves the life out of the soul
leaves you gasping;
with bated breath and a jarred mind

you are left alone
in a vacant mind
lying on the death bed
reminiscing the day love embraced you
around a summer bonfire

now loneliness bounces off
sepia-tinged walls
death draped in pristine
white sheets sitting
at the foot of the bed

scoops its share
masticating life
leaving you rotten
like an empty room with chipped off walls
forgotten and waiting for its due

vacant mind begets explanation
in the hollowness of the night
when the wheezing and choking
cleaves your soul
leaves you asunder

It rattles your mind
you struggle with the existential truth
as this insane "new normal" renders
dying alone a new meaning.

Repainting

By Tim Taylor

In the time of pestilence
life goes on, but smaller;
confined in shrinking spaces,
curling in upon itself.
Revolving in cramped spirals
the stuff of it is squeezed
and twisted, all its colours
are wrung out and washed away.

Yet it endures: one day
the cloud will disappear,
the barricades be lifted.
Those who are left will watch
through blinking eyes as life's
discoloured, crumpled fabric
opens up, unfolds its faded
scenes of brown and grey.

A time for restoration,
an opportunity – perhaps
a duty – not to settle
for what was, but dip the brush
in brighter colours, sweep bold lines
across the canvas of the world,
to paint our future in rich shades
of purple, green and gold.

Emergence

By Tim Taylor

Like stunted trees huddled against a storm
we have grown inwards, in protected space.
What was once punishment is now the norm:
each of us makes a prison of the place
we call our home, warily creeping out
only for reason of necessity.
When promised freedom, we are racked with doubt.
How strange, unsettling it feels, to see
the doors of houses opening like flowers.
We still cling to our reassuring chains,
scared to reclaim the world that once was ours.
Worries and 'what if's echo in our brains,
but it is time to win back what was lost.
I step outside, keeping my fingers crossed.

An Ordinary Day - 1348

By Tim Taylor

An ordinary day:
no portentous thunderstorms
attend the coming of an ordinary ship
into a normal harbour.
Upon the ship, among the ordinary barrels,
jars and boxes, secreted
in their sly but ordinary way
the small, unpaying passengers
that carry, in their smooth black fur
yet smaller, ordinary fleas
who in their turn bear microscopic guests:
not quite so ordinary.
A sailor bends to lift a bale of cloth
and, cursing, staggers with it to the dock.
He lowers it and rests.
Glad to be unburdened of its weight
he smiles, wipes his brow
and stoops to scratch an itch upon his leg.
An ordinary man,
already passing into history.

An Ordinary Day - 1348 was first published in *Up!* Magazine

The Ark Returns

By Michelle M. Tokarczyk

The animals are sluggish.
Their instincts wet-rotted.

The lizards can't camouflage.
The wolves can't find a scent.
The camels are confused by their humps' sway.
The snakes stretch out, hoping for legs.

Two by two, Noah prods them down the plank.
His own feet struggle to balance on dry land,
as his eyes adjust to daylight unfiltered by rain,
as he surveys the drying future before him.
Where to begin when your space is everywhere?

His family waves goodbye to its strange boarders.
Gathers tools, pots, clothes. Remind themselves
of things that humans use, like arms and words.
How do you hug, hold hands?
How do you tell a story?

They gather, so grateful they've been chosen.
So grateful to be alive. But after so many days
sealed in, tumbling like a barrel in falls. . .
God came again.   Spoke of a Covenant.
Promised He'd never drown the world again.
Do we believe Him?

Corona from the Window

By Alicia Viguer-Espert

I watched a masked old man pass by my window
Worries crowded his forehead.
At that light changing hour
A capricious sun abandoned some of its rays
On the deserted street
Snagged on wrought iron gates, windowsills,
The canopies of jacaranda trees.

This dance didn't last,
Eventually, rays tore themselves upwards,
Disappeared without a sound.

I continued seated behind the glass,
A large coyote moved slowly, looking ahead,
Followed by two skinny ones,
Miraculous flapping lifted crows
from the power lines.

A pattern of redness covered the skin of clouds,
Reminded me of a flowery dress
Woven in my city
Where silkworms made it prosper.
In that city
One could admire splendorous brocades
Still worn by women during festivities.
Until a plague killed the Mulberry trees,
Their way of life,
Like today.

I try to read
The old man's concerns stenciled on his forehead
While families, I don't see, count small bills,
Fearful,
Will we have a meal next week?
Who will die?
I wonder whether the planet will heal
and wealth's distribution even out,
Want to champion transparency
for air and water when it's over.

It gives me hope to notice
Groups of women taking the lead
So, we could survive, thrive,
together.

COVID19 Dream

By Mike Wilson

Sleeping head to foot in rows of cots with
partners in another lifetime
                                    a vise grip
near my breastbone lock-jaws my lungs
my chest won't rise
                        black ocean of double
pneumonia pulling me down
without making a sound
a mentor says that since I prayed
in Himalayan caves, I'm blessed with the
wound of an open mind, an easy place for
trouble to nest
                        I sit up

    virus is mental before it's physical:
    I *will* the pliers to let loose of my heart.

Coronavirus Sonnet

By Mike Wilson

Name me after the envelope of stars,
think of me as a blow that blows through you
until your eyes unshut enough to see
change arranged by chance catastrophe.

For some, I'll be the gangplank off a ship,
a door to seeing life surpassing death,
proof existence never stops existing –
ignorance was the only thing ever in peril.

For others, I'm a flag to rally round,
a dipstick measuring depths of selfishness.
Quarantines can never contain me
any more than you contain yourself.

Pandemic is synchronicity,
apocalypse an opportunity.

The Title Poem

O, Captain!

After Walt Whitman

By Kalpana Singh-Chitnis

You cannot blame it all on June gloom,
sitting in your living room, surfing channels
watching plague, politics, and war.

I turn the TV off and read Whitman—
"O, Captain! my Captain!..."
"O the bleeding drops of red..."

I can't wait for the sun to arrive in the eastern hemisphere.
The night sails like a mammoth ship in dark rivers, scooping the dead.
My father, mother, sister, and brother are ailing. Friends have left too soon.

Hark! I hear the faint moaning of the cities shackled from afar.
The buildings hang from the sky lifeless, their tongues out the windows.
The doors are closed, but the oxygen has escaped.

There aren't enough shrouds and wood left in the market.
Like doctors, nurses and essential staff, the forests working
around the clock are making oxygen, coffins, and kindle for cremation.

The animals on the graves appear orphaned. Their masters have left.
The banyan trees stand humble in the country carrying clay pots
hanging from their necks, like the *Bhistis* offering water

to the thirsty souls wandering in the state of *Bardo.*
Shiva roams with his third eye open
in villages and towns and charnel grounds,

emitting fire from the center of his brows,
lighting pyres of the abandoned on river beds,
drinking toxins, flowing in the water to purify the rivers.

Covered in ashes amidst the embers flying,
he contains the spread. He does not exhale.
He is blue, turning darker blue.

The Himalayas melt in grief.
The Ganges widens her shores.
There are more pyres on the ground tonight than stars lit in the sky.

The truth sounds like a lie. But it isn't.
There aren't enough beds and oxygen in the hospitals.
There aren't enough vaccines and medical supplies.

Who is accountable? Who is accountable?
Who is accountable? I beg for help—
help the helpless!

Friends, who couldn't come forward have promised,
they will forward my plea to the rich *NRIs*.
A slap, right in my face!

For the first time, I'm angry
for not being wealthy enough like Gates,
to help my country breathe with one fat check.

Why do I worry? Thirty-three million gods will take care of everything.
Why do I bother? 1.36 billion people will manage their country.
O sister, you will be okay. O Mother, try to sleep now.

I shall breathe for you with my lungs expanded to the continents.
Hope isn't a luxury, it is a necessity.
I invite the *Bell* and sit in silence.

I write an alphabet on a piece of paper and repeat,
until it burns a hole in my heart.
O for Oxygen, O for Oxygen, O for Oxygen.

"O, Captain! my Captain! rise up and hear the bells."

A poem in the wake of the deadly second wave of COVID-19

**Bardo – A transitional state between death and rebirth. *Shiva – A Hindu deity*
*of Annihilation and Purification. *NRIs - Non-Resident Indians. *Bhistis – A tribe*
*of Traditional water bearers in India and Pakistan. *Bell – Meditation Bell*

"But what does it mean, the plague? It's life, that's all."

Albert Camus, *The Plague*

Contributors' Bio Notes

Kelli Russell Agodon and **Melissa Studdard** are poets finding connection in quarantine through collaboration. Poems from their series, *The Daily Wave,* have been published in *Seattle Review of Books, Berfrois,* the UK's *Inspiration in Isolation,* and Stanford University's *Life in Quarantine: Witnessing Global Pandemic.* As well, their collaboration was the focus of Catherine Lu's Grammy-nominated PBS/NPR episode "Meet the Queens of Quarantine Poetry." When they Zoom together, they like to wear funny hats.

Dee Allen: African-Italian performance poet based in Oakland, California. Active on creative writing & Spoken Word tips since the early 1990s. Author of 5 books [*Boneyard, Unwritten Law, Stormwater and Skeletal Black,* all from POOR Press, and from Conviction 2 Change Publishing, *Elohi Unitsi*] and 38 anthology appearances [including Your *Golden Sun Still Shines, Rise, Extreme, The Land Lives Forever, Civil Liberties United, Colossus*: *Home, 2020: The Year That ChangedAmerica, Geography Is Irrelevant from York,* England's own Stairwell Books and the newest from Flower Song Press, created for the 2021 Rio Grande Valley International Poetry Festival, *Boundless*] under his figurative belt so far.

Lana Hechtman-Ayers makes her home in an Oregon coastal town of more cows than people. As managing editor at three small presses, she has shepherded over eighty poetry collections into print. She holds MFAs in Poetry and in Writing Popular Fiction, as well as degrees in Mathematics and Psychology. Her work appears in numerous print and online literary journals, as well as in her nine poetry collections and a romantic time travel novel. Visit her online at LanaAyers.com.

Lopa Banerjee is an author, poet, translator, editor with seven critically acclaimed books and five anthologies in fiction and poetry. She lives in Dallas, Texas where she teaches Creative Writing at Texas Christian University and at OLLI, University of North Texas (UNT). Her poetry has been published in renowned platforms, including 'Life in Quarantine,' the Digital Humanities Archive of Stanford University. She has been a Featured Poet at Rice University, Houston, in November 2019. Besides, she has co-produced and acted in the critically acclaimed poetry film 'Kolkata Cocktail' (2019).

Phyllis Becker is the coordinator of the Riverfront Reading series in Kansas City, Missouri. Her book, *How I Came to Love Jazz* and other Poems, was published in 2008 (Helicon Nine, Editions). Two of her poems have been set to jazz on the compact disc, *Poetry of Love,* produced by jazz vocalist Angela Hagenbach. She has a book forthcoming book from Scapegoat Press in 2022. She has extensive experience in juvenile justice reform and is a Senior Fellow with the Full Frame Initiative, a national social change organization. Phyllis and her husband Mark are jazz enthusiasts and dedicated porch sitters.

Smeetha Bhoumik is a poet, artist, editor and Founder of Women Empowered-India (WE). Smeetha's poetry features in national & international anthologies & publications, and her art, mainly the 'Universe Series,' has been shown in exhibitions in India and abroad.

Ronda Piszk Broatch is the author of Lake of Fallen Constellations (MoonPath Press 2015). Ronda's current manuscript was a finalist with the Charles B. Wheeler Prize and Four Way Books Levis Prize. She is the recipient of an Artist Trust GAP Grant. Ronda's journal publications include Blackbird, 2River View, Sycamore Review, Missouri Review, Palette Poetry, and Public Radio KUOW's *All Things Considered.*

Wendy Taylor Carlisle lives and writes in the Arkansas Ozarks. She is the author of four books and five chapbooks and is the 2020 winner of the Phillip H. McMath Post-Publication Award for *The Mercy of Traffic.* See other work in P*ersimmon Tree, pacificREVIEW*, The Atlanta Review and others. In June, Doubleback Books reprinted her 2008 book, *Discount Fireworks,* as a free download.

Carol Casey lives in Blyth, Ontario, Canada. Her work has been nominated for the Pushcart Prize and has appeared in *The Prairie Journal, The Anti-Languorous Project, Please See Me, Front Porch Review, Cypress, Vita Brevis, Blue Unicorn* and others, including a number of anthologies, most recently, *We Are One: Poems From the Pandemic and the TL;DR Hope Anthology.*

Neelam Saxena Chandra has authored five novels, one novella, fourteen children's books, eight short story collections, and thirty five poetry collections. A bilingual author, she writes in English and Hindi. She has published over 2000 poems and stories in various journals, anthologies, and magazines. She holds the Limca Book of Records, 2015, for being an author with the highest number of publications in a year in English and Hindi. She has won several national and international awards. She was listed in Forbes (India) as one of the most popular 78 authors in 2014.

Liz Chang was 2012 Montgomery County Poet Laureate in Pennsylvania. Her poems have appeared in *Verse Daily, Rock & Sling, Origins Journal, Breakwater Review and Stoneboat Literary Journal,* among others. Her first essay was recently published in Oyster River Pages. Her fiction is forthcoming from Opia. She is an Associate Professor of English at Delaware County Community College.

Cheran – Cheran Rudhramoorthy is a Tamil Canadian academic, poet, playwright, and journalist. He is a professor at the University of Windsor in Canada. He has authored over fifteen books in Tamil, and his work has been translated into twenty languages. Several volumes of his work have been published in English translation. Dr.Cheran is the recipient of the International Poetry Award (2017) from ONV Kurup Foundation in Dubai. He has performed his poetry at various International Writers' festivals in the U.K., Singapore, the U.S., Indonesia, India, Sweden, the Netherlands, Canada, Ramallah, West Bank, Dubai, and Mexico. His plays in the English language have been produced and performed in Toronto, Canada, New York, Chicago, New Jersey, and Singapore. Samples of his works in performance can be found at: www.arcpublications.co.uk/books/cheran-in-a-time-of-burning-488 and www.chowk.sg/the-second-sunrise

Kai Coggin (she/her) is the author of four poetry collections, most recently MINING FOR STARDUST (FlowerSong Press 2021) and INCANDESCENT (Sibling Rivalry Press 2019). She is a queer woman of color who thinks Black Lives Matter, a teaching artist in poetry with the Arkansas Arts Council, and the host of the longest running consecutive weekly open mic series in the country—Wednesday Night Poetry. Recently awarded the 2021 Governor's Arts Award and named "Best Poet in Arkansas" by the Arkansas Times, her fierce and powerful poetry has been nominated four times for The Pushcart Prize, as well as Bettering American Poetry 2015, and Best of the Net 2016 and 2018. Her poems have appeared or are forthcoming in POETRY, Cultural Weekly, SOLSTICE, Bellevue Literary Review, Entropy, SWWIM, Split This Rock, Sinister Wisdom, Lavender Review, Luna Luna, Blue Heron Review, Tupelo Press, West Trestle Review, and elsewhere. Coggin is Associate Editor at The Rise Up Review. She lives with her wife and their two adorable dogs in the valley of a small mountain in Hot Springs National Park, Arkansas.

Candice Louisa Daquin is Senior Editor at Indie Blu(e) Publishing and a Psychotherapist. Indie Blu(e)'s anthology SMITTEN won finalist in the National Indie Excellence Awards and The Kali Project, a collection of Indian women's poetry has just published worldwide. Daquin's poetry is available in most bookstores and she is a long-time animal rights advocate and vegetarian.

Ed Davis has immersed himself in writing and contemplative practices since retiring from college teaching. *Time of the Light*, a poetry collection, was released by Main Street Rag Press in 2013. His latest novel, *The Psalms of Israel Jones* (West Virginia University Press 2014), won the Hackney Award for an unpublished novel in 2010. Many of his stories, essays and poems have appeared in anthologies and journals such as *Leaping Clear, Metafore, Hawaii Pacific Review, and Bacopa Literary Review*. He lives with his wife in the bucolic village of Yellow Springs, Ohio, where he bikes, hikes, meditates and reads religiously.

Annie Finch's six volumes of poetry include *Eve, Calendars* (finalist for the National Poetry Series), *Spells: New and Selected Poems*, and *Among the Goddesses* (Sarasvati Award from ASWM, 2012). She has also published translation, feminist criticism, and the anthologies *A Formal Feeling Comes: Poems in Form* by Contemporary Women, Villanelles, and *Choice Words: Writers on Abortion*. Her poems have appeared on stage at Carnegie Hall and in The *Penguin Book of Twentieth-Century American Poetry*. She holds a B.A. from Yale and Ph.D. from Stanford and was awarded the Robert Fitzgerald Award for her lifetime contribution to the study of Versification.

Linda McCauley Freeman is the author of the full-length poetry collection *The Family Plot* (Backroom Window Press, 2022) and has been widely published in international journals, including in a Chinese translation. She was nominated for a Pushcart Prize 2021. Recently she appeared in Delta Poetry Review, Poet Magazine, Amsterdam Quarterly, and won Grand Prize in StoriArts'Maya Angelou poetry contest. She was selected by the Arts MidHudson for Poets Respond to Art 2020 and 2021 shows and was a three-time winner in the Talespinners Short Story contest judged by Michael Korda. She has an MFA from

Bennington College and is the former poet-in-residence of the Putnam Arts Council. She lives in the Hudson Valley, NY. Follow her at www.Facebook.com/LindaMcCauleyFreeman

Kelsey Goeres is a poet and journalist in the San Francisco Bay Area. She writes about culture, entertainment, and what it means to be a human being. Recently, her poems can be found in *The Dillydoun Review, Brave Voices Magazine,* and *{M}aganda Magazine.* She can be found on Twitter @kelsgore.

Amata Natasha Goldie is an Australian poet and author. Her poems are woven around the central themes of love, unity, consciousness and our eternal nature. She has written unpublished collections of spiritual poetry, prose and soul affirmations. You can find more of her offerings online at Ashram of the Ethers.

Marci Hannewald is a writer, creative seeker, and truthteller based in Ann Arbor, Michigan. She's been pushing boundaries and asking why since the tender age of two and is an unabashed champion for all manner of curious humans who question the status quo in pursuit of balance and a happier, healthier lifestyle. When she's not learning to renavigate the world through Zoom screens and online courses, you'll find her hiking through her local nature preserve bonding with chipmunks and other four-legged creatures. You can learn more about her at marcihannewald.com or say hello at walkingthispath@gmail.com

Sarita Jenamani is an Austria-based poet of Indian origin, a literary translator, anthologist, editor of a bilingual magazine for migrant literature – *Words & Worlds* – a human rights activist, a feminist and general secretary of PEN International's Austrian chapter. She has so far been published in three collections of poetry. English is the chief medium of her creative process. The other two languages she writes in are; Odia, her mother tongue and German. She uses these languages for the translation projects that she undertakes from time to time. Jenamani has translated Rose Ausländer, a leading Austrian poet, and an anthology of contemporary Austrian Poetry from German into Hindi and Odia, respectively. She has received many literary fellowships in Germany and in Austria, including those of the prestigious organizations of 'Heinrich Böll Foundation' and 'Künstlerdorf Schöppingen.'

David Kann is a professor of English, emeritus at Californian Polytechnic State University at San Luis Obispo. His chapbook, "The Language of the Farm" won the Five Oaks Press prize in 2015. Three subsequent chapbooks, "At Fernald School," "Blues for Pip" and "Notes on the Creation" have been published by Finishing Line Press. His poems have appeared in journals such as "Lunch Ticket," "Forge," and "Fourth River.

Alfred K. LaMotte has authored three volumes of poetry with Saint Julian Press. He has co-authored three books of artwork and poetry with Hawaiian artist and spiritual teacher, Rashani Réa. An interfaith college chaplain, meditation teacher, and instructor in World Religions, with degrees from Yale University and Princeton Theological Seminary, he lives on the shore of the Salish Sea, near Seattle, WA, with his wife Anna.

Andrea Livingston's poems have appeared in *The MacGuffin, MockingHeart Review, Rust + Moth,* the *2020 Marin Poetry Center Anthology, Sky Island Journal, Rise Up Review, Paterson Literary Review,* and elsewhere. Her poem "Paper Cranes" received honorable mention in the Barbara Mandigo Kelly Poetry Contest of the Nuclear Age Peace Foundation. She lives in the San Francisco Bay Area, where she works as a public policy editor and writer.

John C. Mannone is a physicist living in Knoxville, Tennessee. His poems appear in *North Dakota Quarterly, Le Menteur, Poetry South, Baltimore Review* and many others. A Jean Ritchie Fellowship winner in Appalachian literature (2017), Mannone served as the celebrity judge for the National Federation of State Poetry Societies (2018). His poetry won the Impressions of Appalachia Creative Arts Contest (2020), as well as awards in fiction and literary nonfiction. His latest of four collections are *Flux Lines* (Linnet's Wings Press) and *Sacred Flute* (Iris Press), both forthcoming in 2022. He edits poetry for *Abyss & Apex* and other journals.

Jennifer Martelli is the author of *My Tarantella* (Bordighera Press), named a "Must Read" by the Massachusetts Center for the Book. Her work has appeared in *Poetry, Thrush*, and *Tahoma Literary Review*. Jennifer Martelli has twice received grants from the Massachusetts Cultural Council. She is a co-poetry editor for *Mom Egg Review*.

Kate Maxwell has been published in Australian and International literary magazines such as *Cordite, Hecate, fourW, Meniscus, Social Alternatives, Brilliant Flash Fiction, Blood and Bourbon*, and *Fiction Kitchen Berlin*. She has also won and been placed in numerous literary awards. She was recently shortlisted for the ACU Poetry Prize. Kate's interests include film, wine, and sleeping. Her first poetry anthology, *Never Good at Maths*, is published with Interactive Publications, Brisbane. She can be found at- https://kateswritingplace.com

Kavita Ezekiel Mendonca was born and raised in a Jewish family in Mumbai. Her first book of poems, 'Family Sunday and other poems', was published in 1989. Her poem, 'How to light up a poem,' has been nominated for a Pushcart Prize. Her Chapbook 'Light of The Sabbath' was recently published on Amazon in September 2021. Kavita's poems have been featured in the Journal of Indian Literature published by Sahitya Akademi, SETU, Harbinger Asylum and The Yearbook of Indian Poetry in English 2020-2021. She has taught English, French, and Spanish in various colleges and schools in India and overseas for over four decades.

Richard Modiano is a native of Los Angeles. From 2010 to 2019, he served as Executive Director of Beyond Baroque Literary/Arts Center. In that time, he produced and curated hundreds of literary events. Richard is a rank and file member of the Industrial Workers of the World. In 2019 he was elected Vice President of the California State Poetry Society. *The Huffington Post* named him as one of 200 people doing the most to promote poetry in the United States.

Antoni Ooto lives and works with his wife, poet/storyteller, Judy DeCroce, in rural upstate New York. Ooto is a well-known abstract expressionist artist whose art is collected throughout the US. Currently, poetry is an additional expression of creativity. His poetry is widely published internationally in print, online journals, and anthologies. Antoni regularly contributes to *The BeZINE, Amethyst Review, Front Porch Review, The Poet Magazine, North of Oxford, OpenDoor Magazine, and Vita Brevis Press.* His poem, *"A Year Without Weight,"* was included in the 2021 anthology BROUGHT TO SIGHT & SWEPT AWAY, which went to number one in New Poetry Anthologies in Amazon.

Nynke Salverda Passi was born and raised in the Netherlands. Her work has been published in *CALYX, Gulf Coast, Red River Review, Illya's Honey,* and *The Anthology of New England Writers*, among other journals. Her poetry has been anthologized in *River of Earth and Sky* and *Pandemic Puzzle Pieces* (Blue Light Press), *Carrying the Branch* (Glass Lyre Press), and *Conestoga Zen* (Conestoga Zen Press). Together with Rustin Larson and Christine Schrum, she is co-editor of the poetry anthology *Leaves by Night, Flowers by Day*. Her story "The Kiss" was nominated for a Pushcart Prize, and her essay "Oom Ealse and the Swan" was a finalist in the 2014 Editor's Prize of The Missouri Review. She is director of the low-residency MFA in Creative Writing at M.I.U. and of The Soul Ajar, offering workshops that intersect writing, creativity, and healing.

Suman Pokhrel is a poet, lyricist, playwright, translator, and artist from Nepal. His poems have been translated into several languages and have appeared in notable journals worldwide. His poetry has been included in the syllabus of literary studies in Indian and Nepali universities. Suman Pokhrel was awarded the SAARC Literary Award in 2013 and 2015.

Anushiya Ramaswamy grew up in Colombo, Sri Lanka and is currently a Professor of English at Southern Illinois University Edwardsville. Anushiya's work has appeared in World Literature Today and Callaloo. She is the translator of the Sri Lankan-born Tamil writer Shobasakthi's novels Gorilla and Traitor as well as a selection of his short stories titles *The MGR Murder Trial.* She has also translated a collection of poetry by the Tamil Dalit poet N.D. Rajkumar, *Give Us This Day A Feast of Flesh* (Navayana Publishers, New Delhi). Anushiya was also one of the three translators of the international poetry collection, I*n Our Translated World: Contemporary Global Tamil Poetry* published in Toronto, Canada by Tamil Literary Garden in 2014.

Mario Rigli is a poet, painter, sculptor, writer, and translator. Born on July 7, 1949, in Terranuova Bracciolini, a small village in Tuscany, Mario is the author of "Laurine," a collection of tales (1985), and "Imaginary Nectar" (poetry collection, 1995). He co-authored "A Ticket To Hell" with his son Philip, published in 1998. In 2013, his poetry collection, "Fragments of the Moon," was translated into Arabic by Nizar Sartawi and published in Jordan in 2018. He is also the author of "Words over the Ocean" (Inner Child Press 2020) and "Quando scaturiscono le parole" (Betti Publisher).

Jeannie E. Roberts lives in Wisconsin, where she writes, draws and paints, and often photographs her natural surroundings. She's authored seven books, five poetry collections and two illustrated children's books. Her newest collection, *As If Labyrinth - Pandemic Inspired Poems*, was released by Kelsay Books in April of 2021. Her poems appear in *Anti-Heroin Chic*, *Sky Island Journal*, *Verse-Virtual*, and elsewhere. She's an animal lover, a nature enthusiast, Best of the Net award nominee, and a poetry editor of the online literary magazine *Halfway Down the Stairs.*

Prof. Nandini Sahu, Professor of English and Former Director, School of Foreign Languages, IGNOU, New Delhi, India, is an established Indian English poet, creative writer and folklorist. She is the author/editor of fifteen books. She is the recipient of the Literary Award/Gold Medal from the hon'ble Vice President of India for her contribution to English Studies. Her areas of research interest cover New Literature, Critical Theory, Folklore and Culture Studies, Children's Literature and American Literature.

Dr. Abhi Subedi is a significant name in Nepali literature. Born on June 30, 1945, in Tehrathum district in Eastern Nepal, and educated in Nepal and Scotland, he has written over four dozen books of poetry, translation, essay, and playwright. He has done several interdisciplinary studies on the subjects of freedom, culture, literature, arts, and social transformations. He was given the "SAARC Literary Award" in 2010 and "Yug Kavi Siddhicharan Award" in 2013. Dr. Subedi had a career as a professor of English literature and the head of the English department at Tribhuvan University for forty years.

Ndaba Sibanda is the author of *Notes, Themes, Things And Other Things, The Gushungo Way, Sleeping Rivers, Love O'clock, The Dead Must Be Sobbing, Football of Fools, Cutting-edge Cache, Of the Saliva and the Tongue, When Inspiration Sings In Silence, The Way Forward, Sometimes Seasons Come With Unseasonal Harvests, As If They Minded: The Loudness Of Whispers, This Cannot Be Happening: Speaking Truth To Power, The Dangers Of Child Marriages: Billions Of Dollars Lost In Earnings And Human Capital, The Ndaba Jamela and Collections* and *Poetry Pharmacy*. Sibanda's work has received Pushcart Prize and Best of the Net nominations. Some of his work has been translated into Serbian.

Ram Krishna Singh, born on 31 December 1950 in Varanasi (Uttar Pradesh, India), has been writing poetry in English for over four decades. A retired Professor (IIT-ISM) and widely translated and published, he has authored more than 20 poetry collections, including the latest AGAINST THE WAVES: SELECTED POEMS (New Delhi: Authors Press) https://pennyspoetry.wikia.com/wiki/R.K._Singh

Donna Snyder has poetry collections published by Chimbarazu, Virgogray, and NeoPoiesis presses. She founded the grassroots literary Tumblewords Project in 1995 and continues to organize its free weekly workshops and other literary events in the borderlands around El Paso, Texas. Her poetry and book reviews appear in a number of anthologies and journals. Her poems are being translated into the Bangla language and will appear in a 'zine in Bangladesh in 2022. She previously practiced law representing indigenous people, people with disabilities, and immigrant workers.

Megha Sood is an award-winning Poet, Editor, Author, Blogger from New Jersey, USA. Recipient of 2021 Poet Fellowship from MVICW (Martha's Vineyard Institute of Creating Writing) and a National Level Winner for the 2020 Spring Mahogany Prize. Associate Editor Literary Journals *Mookychick* (UK), *Life and Legends* (USA), and Literary Partner with "Life in Quarantine," Stanford University. Author of Chapbook ("My Body is Not an Apology," Finishing Line Press, 2021) and Full Length ("My Body Lives Like a Threat," FlowerSongPress (2022).She blogs at https://meghasworldsite.wordpress.com/ and tweets at - @meghasood16.

Tim Taylor lives in Meltham, West Yorkshire, UK. His poems have appeared in various magazines (e.g., *Acumen, Orbis, Pennine Platform, The Lake*) and anthologies. He was second in the Hammond House International Poetry Competition 2020 and has won, or been shortlisted in several other competitions. Tim's first collection, Sea Without a Shore, was published in 2019 by Maytree Press; he has also had two novels published by Crooked Cat. Tim teaches Ethics at Leeds University and enjoys playing the guitar and walking up hills. https://timwordsblog.wordpress.com/

Michelle Tokarczyk's poetry has been published in many other journals and anthologies; including *The Literary Review, The Skinny Poetry Journal, the minnesota review, Earth's Daughters, For a Living: The Poetry of Work* (anthology), and *Only the Sea Keeps: Poetry of the Tsunami* (anthology). She was born and raised in a working-class family in New York City. After completing a doctorate in English, she taught for many years in a college in Baltimore. Now retired, she lives and works full-time in New York City.

Alicia Viguer-Espert was raised with the culture, traditions and love of and for the Mediterranean people. For her, old and new experiences combine in the never-ending lesson of living, opening new avenues for hope and understanding in her poetry. Her work has been published in national and international presses, and she has been the featured poet at numerous venues. Winner of the San Gabriel Valley Poetry Contest with "Holding a Hummingbird," her second chapbook, "Out of the Blue Womb of the Sea," was published by Four Feathers Press. She's a Pushcart nominee.

Mike Wilson's work has appeared in magazines including *Cagibi Literary Journal, Stoneboat, The Aurorean,* and *The Ocotillo Review*, and in Mike's book, *Arranging Deck Chairs on the Titanic*, (Rabbit House Press, 2020), political poetry for a post-truth world. He received the Kentucky State Poetry Society's Chaffin/Kash Prize in 2019. Mike resides in Central Kentucky, USA, summers in ecstasy, winters in despair, and can be found at mikewilsonwriter.com

Forthcoming

From River Paw Press

www.riverpawpress.com

Forthcoming

From River Paw Press

www.riverpawpress.com

Kalpna Singh-Chitnis is a Pushcart Prize nominated, award-winning Indian-American poet, writer, filmmaker, and author of four poetry collections. Her works have appeared in notable journals such as *World Literature Today, Columbia Journal, California Quarterly, Indian Literature, Silk Routes Project* (IWP) at The University of Iowa, Stanford University's *Life in Quarantine,"* etc. Her works have been translated into fourteen languages.

Poems from her award-winning book *Bare Soul* and her poetry film "River of Songs" have been included in the "Nova Collection" and the "Polaris Collection" Lunar Codex time capsules going on the Moon with NASA's "Nova-C lander missions to Oceanus Procellarum" in Spring 2022 and "NASA VIPER" rover mission to the Lunar South Pole in 2023. Kalpna's poetry has received praise from eminent writers, such as Nobel Prize in Literature nominee Dr. Wazir Agha, Vaptsarov Award, and Ordre des Arts et des Lettres recipient Amrita Pritam, and poet and Academy Award winning lyricist, and filmmaker Gulzar. A former lecturer of Political Science, Kalpna Singh-Chitnis is also the Editor-in-Chief of *Life and Legends*, the Translation Editor of *IHRAF WRITES*, and an Advocacy Member of the United Nations Association of the USA. She holds a degree in Film Directing from the NYFA and works as an independent filmmaker in Hollywood. Her next poetry collection *Trespassing My Ancestral Land* and is in the making. Website: www.kalpnasinghchitnis.com, @Accesskalpna

www.ingramcontent.com/pod-product-compliance
Lightning Source LLC
Chambersburg PA
CBHW021739190726

48288CB00009B/3113